Going for the Gold

A Parent's Playbook for Behavior Change

W. Jean Cronin, Ph.D.

Linda M. Bessire, Ed.D.

Edited by Sandra L. Knauke
Cover design and text layout by Leslie Spencer Prassas
Production assistance by Denise Geddis

ISBN 1-57035-520-7

Printed in the United States of America

Published and Distributed by

SOPRIS
WEST

4093 Specialty Place • Longmont, CO 80504 • (303) 651-2829
www.sopriswest.com

165GOLD/6-02/C&M/.75M/217

About the Authors

W. Jean Cronin, Ph.D.

Dr. Cronin has worked with children and families in a variety of settings. While completing her doctorate at Loyola University of Chicago, Dr. Cronin specialized in neuropsychology, completing a practicum at Evanston Hospital and a predoctorate and postdoctorate internship at Loyola University Medical Center. In those settings, she worked with children with neurological involvement, including traumatic brain injury, cancer, epilepsy, spina bifida, autism, Asperger's Disorder, severe emotional disturbance, learning disabilities, and ADHD. She also worked with a specialized foster care program in rural Nebraska, teaching parents and staff how to create and carry out specific, positive plans to teach appropriate behavior to children and adolescents with significant behavior problems. For the past seven years, Dr. Cronin has been a psychologist in Las Vegas, Nevada, with the sixth largest school district in the United States. She is serving a second term as Nevada's delegate to the National Association of School Psychologists (NASP).

Linda M. Bessire, Ed.D.

Dr. Bessire's work with children includes raising two children and a lifetime of education and counseling. For the past seven years, she has worked as an administrator of school psychologists, special education, and general education. Before becoming an administrator, Dr. Bessire had professional experience teaching mathematics and Spanish, work-

ing as a high school guidance counselor, serving as a liaison between community mental health services and the school on behalf of children with behavior disorders, and providing psychoeducational services to parents and students as a school psychologist. She has also worked with children and parents in private practice at a psychiatric clinic. Dr. Bessire holds a doctorate in educational administration and leadership from Kansas State University and graduate degrees in both school psychology and counseling.

Contents

Preface

Over many years of working with children and their families, we have been touched by the immense desire that parents have to do what is best for their children. However, many factors interfere with their ability to do so.

The media and entertainment industries provide many different, sometimes subtle, messages about values through books and movies. Children are often exposed to aggression and violence as ways of problem solving. Family schedules are increasingly hectic. In many families, both parents work. Often, single parents struggle alone. In addition, parents must find child care, schedule activities, and meet the family's needs and wants. There is too much to do in too little time. Often, there is no time for relaxing and bonding.

When parents experience difficulties with their children's behavior, it adds more stress. Parents often seek advice from relatives, friends, professionals, or parenting books. Almost everyone is willing to offer suggestions. However, we have seen a large gap between parents knowing what to do and their ability to apply this knowledge. We have also noticed that parents rarely have a long-term goal.

We wrote this guide to fill this gap. Most parenting or behavior books are overwhelming because they contain so much information. Parents may understand some points but still not be able to develop a long-term plan. As the comedian Rita Rudner said about great sounding, but complicated, recipes: "That's not going to happen!"

We provide just enough information to explain how to become more effective at parenting. Our focus is not just on what to do but, more importantly, on how to do it. The purpose of this guide is to help parents understand the basics of behavior and learn how to improve family relationships. It is not meant to provide volumes of information. Instead, our intent is to provide the knowledge and the skills necessary for changing behavior and improving relationships between parents and children. This guide will help parents accomplish these goals in a way that is fun for both parents and children.

Most children and adults love to play games. Research shows that children learn best when they are fully involved and having fun. The information in this guide is presented in a game-like format where parents assume the role of coaches, teaching their children the plays they need to be effective participants in their lives today, and ultimately, as adults.

In our fields of school psychology and education, we have successfully used the plan in this guide to help children learn appropriate behavior. The steps of this plan have also been used successfully for years by parents, educators, psychologists, and other people who work with children. By understanding the basics of behavior, parents will have the tools needed to manage difficult behavior in a positive way. The Game Plan used in this guide organizes the tried-and-true principles of behavior management into a simple, usable method.

We hope this guide provides parents with a way of thinking about behavior that will guide their long-term thinking and their daily actions. This guide is easy to use, it is fun for parents and children, and it will work! It is unique in its simplicity—providing the basics for understanding and changing behavior. Although you need an initial investment of time and energy to set up the plan, the long-term benefits will be less time and energy spent dealing with misbehavior. By following this guide, parents will have a plan to follow at all times, which removes the stress of making decisions in difficult situations. Over time, using the plan should become automatic, which means less stress over inappropriate behavior and more time for positive family interactions and growth.

Introduction

Parents need to do more than just "understand": they need to know how to change what is going on in their families.

— Gerald R. Patterson, *Living With Children*

Dealing with inappropriate behavior can be challenging with any child at times. Some children are more difficult to parent, however, and what typically works to correct behavior with other children is not effective. As problem behaviors continue, family interactions can become very negative, resulting in more of the misbehavior. At this point, emotions and power struggles take over. Reasoning and bargaining have little or no impact, and change becomes quite difficult. Even though you may be able to readily acquire knowledge about behavior, applying that knowledge can be a struggle. Books, tapes, counseling, or workshops usually do not result in long-term improvement. Add a busy schedule with limited time and the result can be anger, fatigue, frustration, and overall feelings of failure.

This guide will help you if you are concerned about your child's behavior. If your child has significant behavior problems, you will learn how to teach a positive behavior, such as remaining calm when upset. This guide will also help if you want to minimize the risk of future behavior problems. The plan can be used by parents and other caregivers—such as grandparents, baby-sitters, and teachers—of children of all ages.

You can use this guide with children who have disabilities, such as Attention Deficit/Hyperactivity Disorder, traumatic brain injury, mental retardation, or emotional disturbance. With a good plan and commitment to the plan, you can change most behavior. For some children, change may take longer, with greater inconsistency in behavior. For example, a child who does not think before acting can still benefit from the program. For all children, however, the inappropriate behavior may reappear. Staying with the plan should reduce the chances of this happening.

Your child's behavior problems should always be discussed with the family doctor, especially if there are significant changes in behavior. In some cases, problem behavior may disappear with medical intervention. For example, irritability may be caused by headaches, allergies, or medications. In cases where medication is necessary to help control behavior, a behavior plan will still help teach appropriate behavior.

This guide is not a replacement for counseling or therapy, although counseling or therapy can be used at the same time as the plan and may be necessary in some cases. For example, some children show problem behaviors, such as extreme anger or withdrawal, during a divorce. Such children may benefit from both a behavior plan and counseling. For children with major, ongoing emotional problems, counseling or therapy and behavior plans are both important.

The Basics of Behavior

CHAPTER 1

The best way to remedy child behavior problems is by encouraging skillful behavior that competes with problematic behavior.

— Elaine A. Blechman, *Solving Child Behavior Problems at Home and at School*

All children need the chance to make choices and experience the consequences, positive or negative, of those choices. You need to give your child the freedom to fail and succeed while providing support and guidance, such as deciding what movies and games are appropriate. Of course, you should get involved if your child is in danger. For example, you might need to stop a fight, pull your child out of the street, or restrict Internet access. The freedom to fail and succeed does not, in other words, mean there are no rules.

Teaching appropriate behavior is important so that children learn the skills they will need as adults. Parents work to earn money for their family and, hopefully, to help their community by providing a service to others. It is the job of children to get an education and be contributing members of their family, so that they will be able to provide for themselves and their loved ones, as well as help their community.

A good behavior plan will help teach appropriate behavior. In this guide, the plan is designed as a game with rewards for appropriate behavior and penalties for inappropriate behavior. Good plans run themselves and remove much of the conflict that develops during difficult situations.

Over a long period of time, a behavior plan will produce positive changes in behavior. As children experience success with one behavior, their other behavior often improves too. Family relationships also get better, because there is less conflict and more success.

Behavior Changes

To make long-term changes in your child's behavior, you should know a little about behavior in general. One basic rule is that

behavior being repeated is somehow being rewarded. In other words, the child gets some kind of payoff for misbehaving. To change behavior, then, you must stop the payoff for inappropriate behavior and reward only the desired behavior. This sounds simple enough, but it can be quite difficult.

You must understand the behavior and invest enough time to change the behavior. In Chapters 2 and 3, you will analyze your child's misbehavior and some of the rewards that your child gets for behaving inappropriately.

Life Is a Game; Childhood Is the Training Camp

Life can be viewed as a game, with rules, that everyone wants to participate in and enjoy. To do their best in school, work, and relationships, children should know the rules of life and follow them. The game of life is played everyday in different places with different people and different rules. Effective participation in different activities requires understanding the different rules. For example, going to church calls for different behavior than visiting an amusement park. Everywhere, however, there is one basic rule: *A person's behavior directly affects what happens to that person.*

Many children quickly learn this rule, either by watching others or being specifically taught, and they follow the rule most of the

time. Some children can control their behavior on their own. Other children need clear, repeated instructions. Others may know this rule but still act without thinking. In addition, there are those who know what to do but choose not to do it.

Part of life is learning the connection between behavior and consequences. People with a good work ethic often work first, then play. Many children try to bargain with play first but then never get around to the work. Teaching them to do the work first, to earn a more enjoyable activity later, is an important idea for them to learn. Delaying an undesirable task only makes it more undesirable as time passes. For example, when children put off doing their homework, they build up a lot of negative emotions by the time they get to it, making it difficult to put positive energy into their work. When children understand this idea, they often begin to *enjoy* getting the undesirable task done before it becomes overwhelming. Eventually, their enjoyment of finishing work will serve as motivation.

This guide will help you teach your child that behavior has consequences. In the behavior plan in this guide, your child will earn privileges, such as watching television or playing with a friend, based on his or her behavior. By connecting the behavior to the result, your child can learn to be an effective player in his or her life today and prepare for a future as an adult.

When your child misbehaves, he or she is being sidelined in the game of life and cannot participate in a positive, meaningful way. The game of life should focus on eager, challenging participation while following the rules that make the game fair for everyone.

I can't image a person becoming a success who doesn't give this game of life everything he's got.

— Walter Cronkite

When things come easily for children, they grow up thinking the world owes them a living.

— H. Stephen Glenn and Jane Nelsen, *Raising Children for Success*

Parents as Coaches

The role of the coach in any game is to:

- Understand the game and the players.
- Develop strategies for the game.
- Complete the game plan.
- Establish a supportive, teaching relationship with the players.

In sports, a coach creates a game plan based on the objectives of the game and the players on the team. The coach is also an example of the determination, persistence, and sportsmanship that players need to stay in the game.

In this guide, parents, relatives, baby-sitters, and other caregivers are all coaches. As the coach, you will use the charts in Chapter 4 to choose the behavior you want your child to learn and create a plan to teach your child that behavior.

It is helpful if all coaches follow the same rules. Consistency reduces confusion and will help your child apply his or her behavior to all situations. In Chapter 5, you'll create rules for the rewards and penalties your child can earn in the game. To keep track of your child's rewards and behavior, you'll use the Scoreboard, which is explained in Chapter 6. Special situations and problems with the game are covered in Chapter 7.

While following the plan, you will also build a positive relationship with your child. Just as children work harder for a favorite teacher, players often work harder for a coach they like. You will learn more about how to improve your relationship with your child in Chapter 8.

The Pregame Analysis for the Player

CHAPTER 2

If you are able to state a problem, then the problem can be solved.

— Edwin Land, Inventor of the Instant Camera

With any problem behavior, it is rarely effective to postpone intervention because of the hope that your child is going through a phase or will grow out of it. During the wait, your child's social interactions and academic progress may be affected. Just as children learning to hit a baseball will benefit from batting practice, children learning appropriate behavior need specific instructions. To help your child change his or her behavior, you should create a plan to teach the behavior you want.

Although there may be several problem behaviors, you should focus on changing one behavior at a time. Often, when you change one behavior, many of your child's other behaviors will also improve.

The first step in creating a plan is to examine the current problems. You will use the **Pregame Analysis** to develop the plan and collect information.

During the Pregame Analysis, you will analyze two behaviors: your child's behavior and your behavior in relation to your child.

In sports, a player is sidelined or benched for mistakes or bad plays. Similarly, your child's problem behaviors can sideline him or her from positive interactions. The more often your child is sidelined, the more opportunities he or she misses. The Pregame Analysis will help you understand the **sideliner** (problem behavior) and how often it happens. In the first part of this analysis, you will examine the sideliner. In the second part, you will count how often the sideliner occurs.

Sideliner Analysis

In order to create a behavior plan, you must first clearly understand the problem behavior. You need to describe the sideliner in simple, observable terms.

Psychologists and educators use the **ABC model** to analyze behavior. In this model, *A* stands for antecedents, *B* stands for the behavior, and *C* stands for consequences. **Antecedents** are what happens before the behavior occurs or what sets the stage for the behavior to occur. **Consequences**—what happens after the behavior occurs—affect whether or not the behavior will occur again.

A simple example of the ABC model is a thirsty child getting a drink of water (see Figure 1). The antecedent, which leads to the behavior, is the thirst. The behavior is drinking the water. The consequence, what happens after the behavior, is that the child is no longer thirsty. Because the consequence was positive, the child will repeat the behavior.

The Sideliner Analysis chart (see Figure 2) used in this guide follows the ABC model. The three steps you will use to fill in the chart match the three parts of the ABC model:

1. Describe the problem behavior in the middle column under "Behavior."

2. List what happens right before the sideliner in the "Antecedents: What Happens Before?" column of the Sideliner Analysis chart. Write down

who is present, who is interacting with the child, when the behavior occurs, and where the behavior occurs. Understanding what happens *before* the behavior occurs will help you make a plan for getting appropriate behavior instead.

3. List the responses to the sideliner in the "Consequences: What Happens After?" column of the Sideliner Analysis chart. Write down how all family members (including you) respond to the behavior. Understanding what happens *after* the behavior occurs is key to getting the desired behavior and stopping accidental reinforcement of the undesired behavior.

In this book, we will use two children with common behavior problems as examples. The first is Resistant Ralph, who does not follow directions. The other is Angry Agnes, who loses control when upset.

ABC Model

Antecedents: What Happens Before?	Behavior	Consequences: What Happens After?
Thirst	Drinking Water	No more thirst

Figure 1

Sideliner Analysis

Player:_____

Date: _____

Antecedents: What Happens Before?	Behavior	Consequences: What Happens After?

Figure 2

Example: Resistant Ralph

On Saturday morning, Ralph's family got up to fix breakfast together. Instead of joining the family, Ralph began watching television as soon as he got up. Ralph ignored his mother's repeated requests to join the family.

When breakfast was ready, Ralph's mother asked him to sit down and eat. Ralph ignored her. She repeated the request several times, each time getting louder and angrier. Ralph finally said that he did not want breakfast so he could finish watching one of his favorite television shows. Ralph's mother told him that he needed to eat and finish his chores so the family could go to the shopping mall.

Ralph replied that he would be there in a minute, but he never came. The family finished breakfast and left Ralph's food on the table. Everyone else began their chores. Ralph's parents repeatedly told Ralph to eat and do his chores so they could leave. Ralph continued to watch television and ignore his parents. Ralph's brother and sister became upset that Ralph was not helping and started to complain.

Ralph's father angrily told Ralph that if he did not finish his chores, he could not go with the family to the mall— where Ralph's favorite computer store was. Finally, Ralph went to the kitchen to eat, but complained that his food was cold. His frustrated mother heated up the food, telling Ralph to hurry so he could get his chores done.

Ralph, meanwhile, took a long time to eat while the rest of the family completed their chores. When everyone else was ready to leave, Ralph was not dressed, had left his messy breakfast dishes on the table, and had not done his chores. To speed things up, Ralph's parents cleaned up his dishes, helped him get dressed, and decided he could do his chores later. His brother and sister were mad because Ralph did not have to do anything. Ralph's parents were furious because Ralph was so slow. Even Ralph was mad because everyone else was mad at him.

The three columns of the Sideliner Analysis chart for Resistant Ralph are filled in as follows:

1. Ralph's problem behavior is written in the "Behavior" column. He did not eat breakfast when asked, do his chores, or get ready to leave for the mall with the rest of the family. Ralph had a problem following directions in a reasonable period of time.

2. What happens before Ralph's sideliner is written in the "Antecedents: What Happens Before?" column. Ralph's parents allowed him to get out of bed and begin watching television without dressing, helping with breakfast, or doing chores. They did not tell him ahead of time what behavior they expected or make sure that the television was never turned on. Ralph's parents tried directions to get Ralph to behave, and Ralph's father did not become involved until everyone was angry. His parents also didn't address his problem behavior. As in many busy families, they did not deal directly with his inappropriate behavior in order to save time.

3. What happens after Ralph's behavior is listed in the "Consequences: What Happens After?" column. Resistant Ralph ignored all requests from his parents and he got to do what he wanted to do, which was watch television. He did not help make breakfast, clean up after himself, or do his chores. He also had help with dressing. Ralph did not follow instructions except for finally eating breakfast when his father threatened not to take him to the mall.

It is likely that this is a pattern of behavior between Ralph and his parents. For Ralph, the payoff for not following instructions was watching television, eating breakfast when he wanted, not doing chores, and getting lots of attention from his parents.

Ralph's completed Sideliner Analysis chart is shown in Figure 3.

Sideliner Analysis

Player: Resistant Ralph

Date: 02/18 – 02/24

Antecedents: What Happens Before?	Behavior	Consequences: What Happens After?
Parents made requests.

Parents did not tell Ralph what they wanted him to do before he started watching television.

There was no television schedule.

Parents gave many reminders and threats. | Not following directions in a reasonable period of time. | Ralph got lots of attention.

Ralph watched one of his television shows.

Ralph did not do his chores.

Ralph didn't get punished for his behavior.

Ralph upset positive family activities.

Ralph was treated differently than his sister and brother. |

Figure 3

Example: Angry Agnes

Agnes was at home on Saturday afternoon with her mother and sister. Agnes's mother was doing laundry and ironing clothes for the upcoming week. Agnes was listening to her CD player and looking at a magazine. Agnes's sister walked by and heard Agnes playing a CD that she had taken from her sister's bedroom without permission. Agnes's sister demanded the CD back from Agnes. Agnes refused, became instantly angry, and began yelling that her sister had more CDs than she had.

When Agnes's mother came to stop the argument, she told Agnes to return the CD to her sister. Agnes became even angrier and began stomping her feet. Agnes's mother told her that both girls were treated the same, but Agnes ignored her and started throwing things across the room. Agnes's sister and mother gave in and let Agnes keep the CD for the day. Agnes immediately calmed down and turned her CD player up louder.

Later that afternoon, Agnes's mother interrupted the two sisters in their rooms. Their grandmother had called needing help. A baby-sitter was coming to stay with the girls. Agnes became angry immediately, said that she hated baby-sitters, and burst out crying. She demanded to go with her mother and yelled about how unfairly she was always treated. When her mother tried to calm her down, Agnes yelled even louder and began crying uncontrollably, gasping for breath. Agnes's mother decided that she could not leave Agnes with a baby-sitter when she was so upset and took her along to her grandmother's. Agnes's sister stayed home with the baby-sitter.

Angry Agnes's Sideliner Analysis chart is filled in as follows:

1. Agnes's problem behavior, losing control when upset, is listed in the "Behavior" column. Agnes became upset, yelled, cried, stomped her feet, and threw a tantrum when she did not get her way.

2. What happens before Agnes's sideliner is written in the "Antecedents: What Happens Before?" column. Agnes was asked to do two things she did not want to do: return a CD that she had borrowed without permission and stay with a baby-sitter. Agnes's mother did not set rules for borrowing and sharing ahead of time. Her mother's attempts to calm Agnes resulted in worse behavior.

3. What happens after Agnes's sideliner is listed in the "Consequences: What Happens After?" column. Agnes got what she wanted; she kept the CD for the rest of the day and she went with her mother instead of staying with a baby-sitter. She calmed down immediately when she got her way.

Figure 4 shows Angry Agnes's completed Sideliner Analysis chart.

Action: Completing the Sideliner Analysis Chart

Like a coach getting ready for a game, you will become an observer and examine your child's behavior problem. During one week (or longer if needed), follow the steps listed below. If you need to, refer back to the examples for help. There is a blank Sideliner Analysis chart in the Appendix of Forms.

1. Write the problem behavior in the "Behavior" column. Be as specific as possible.

Sideliner Analysis

Player: _Angry Agnes_

Date: _07/18 – 07/24_

Antecedents:
What Happens Before?

Mother made requests.

There were no rules for borrowing and sharing.

Mother's attempts at calming caused Agnes to get even angrier.

Behavior

Losing control when upset.

Consequences:
What Happens After?

Agnes received lots of attention.

Agnes did not do the things she did not want to do and she got to do what she wanted to do.

There were no consequences for Agnes's behavior.

Agnes upset family interactions.

Agnes was treated differently than her sister.

Figure 4

2. Examine what happens before the problem behavior occurs and write it in the "Antecedents: What Happens Before?" column. Note any patterns, such as "who," "what," "where," and "when."

3. Observe what happens after the sideliner occurs and write it in the "Consequences: What Happens After?" column.

Frequency of the Sideliner

Once you have completed the first part of the Player Analysis, you have identified and examined your child's sideliner. Now, you need to count the sideliner for one week to find out how often it happens. Knowing how often the sideliner happens will help you decide how often you need to use rewards in the behavior plan. This information will also help you measure how well the plan is working.

To count the sideliner, you can make a mark on a calendar or an index card. You can also put masking tape on your sleeve and make a mark each time the sideliner occurs. At the end of each day, you record the total number of marks for the day on the Frequency of Sideliner chart. There is a blank copy of this chart in the Appendix of Forms.

Your child will probably notice that you are watching his or her behavior. At this point, however, do not explain what is happening and do not change how you or other care-givers deal with the behavior.

While counting how often the sideliner happens, you may learn more about the antecedents and consequences of the sideliner. Add this new information to the Sideliner Analysis chart.

The completed Frequency of Sideliner charts for Resistant Ralph and Angry Agnes are shown in Figures 5 and 6. Resistant Ralph's parents counted his behavior for one week to

Frequency of Sideliner

Player: _Resistant Ralph_

Week of: _02/18 – 02/24_

Day of Week	Monday	Tuesday	Wednesday	Thursday	Friday	Saturday	Sunday
Total	8	3	6	10	4	15	18

Figure 5

see how many times a day Ralph did not follow directions the first time they were given. From the chart, you can see that Ralph's sideliner was a problem during the whole week, occurring the most on Thursday, Saturday, and Sunday.

Angry Agnes's mother counted her behavior for one week to see how many times a day Agnes did not stay calm when upset. The chart shows that there was usually one sideliner a day, with more at the end of the week and on the weekend.

Action: Completing the Frequency of Sideliner Chart

Use the Frequency of Sideliner chart in the Appendix and count the sideliner using the following steps for at least one week:

1. Each time the sideliner happens during the day, make a mark on a calendar, notecard, or masking tape on a sleeve.

2. Count the number of times the sideliner happened each day, and write the total on the Frequency of Sideliner chart.

If you want, you can observe the behavior (using the Sideliner Analysis chart) and count the behavior (using the Frequency of Sideliner chart) at the same time. You do not have to complete the Sideliner Analysis chart before beginning the Frequency of Sideliner chart. You may, however, find it less confusing to do one chart at a time. Keep both of these charts available to use when making the behavior plan.

Frequency of Sideliner

Player: _Angry Agnes_

Week of: _02/18 – 02/24_

Day of Week	Monday	Tuesday	Wednesday	Thursday	Friday	Saturday	Sunday
Total	1	1	0	2	3	5	4

Figure 6

The Pregame Analysis for the Coach

CHAPTER 3

To learn more about how you behave with your child, you should actually count and record how you talk to and work with your child each day. When you and your child are busy and involved in everyday activities, you may not be aware of the tone of your communications. Habits form and become automatic. It takes a conscious effort to pay attention to patterns and analyze them.

During the Coach Analysis, you, as a coach, will record the number of times you (or other caregivers) give your child **recognition** or **zingers** (criticism) throughout the day. You should record *any* recognition or zinger, not just those connected to the problem behavior.

In order to do the Coach Analysis effectively, you need to understand exactly what recognition and zingers are. What could be recognition to an adult might be a zinger to a child. Recognition is any time that your child receives positive, supportive feedback. Recognition can be verbal (spoken) or shown through behavior. With verbal recognition, you give specific information about the positive behavior. For example, "Thank you for picking up your shoes," "Good job cleaning your room," or "Way to go! You finished all of your homework before bedtime."

Nonverbal (unspoken) recognition includes a positive tone of voice, nods of approval, and smiles.

A zinger or criticism is any negative statement made either with words or behavior. For example, "You make me so mad," "Why did you do that," or "You didn't do that right!" Unspoken zingers include speaking sarcastically, narrowing the eyes, glaring, stomping away, and throwing things. Sometimes the words are positive, but the tone of the voice changes the meaning. For example, the words *great job* take on a different meaning if your voice is loud or angry.

Action: Completing the Frequency of Recognition/Zingers Chart

Recognition and zingers should be counted for one week. You can limit the counting to times each day when there is a lot of interaction between you and your child. In this case, note the times when you do the counting. If you count during only parts of the day, you should vary the times somewhat. It is also a good idea for each parent or caregiver to count their own or each other's recognition and zingers, as there may be differences from person to person. The chart used for recording recognition and zingers is the Frequency of Recognition/Zingers chart located in the Appendix of Forms and shown in Figure 7.

To complete the Frequency of Recognition/Zingers chart, follow these steps:

1. Each day, keep a count of recognition and zingers on a calendar, index card, or masking tape on a sleeve. Do not count the recognition and zingers that the child gives you.

2. At the end of each day, write the total count of recognition and zingers on the Frequency of Recognition/Zingers chart.

3. At the end of the week, write the total number of recognitions and the total number of zingers. Compare the two totals, and note the differences. Are you more positive or more negative when you are with your child?

You have now finished the Pregame Analysis and completed three charts: the Sideliner Analysis, the Frequency of Sideliner, and the Frequency of Recognition/Zingers. You will use these charts to create the Game Plan, which is discussed in the next chapter.

Frequency of Recognition/Zingers

Coach: _____

Player: _____

Week of: _____

	Monday	Tuesday	Wednesday	Thursday	Friday	Saturday	Sunday	Total
Recog- nition								
Zingers								

Figure 7

The First and Second Positive Behavior Boosters

Expecting children to obey also involves having a plan for what you are going to do if they don't. In fact, the secret to virtually frustration-free discipline is, first, have a plan; then, carry it through consistently.

— John Rosemond, *Six-Point Plan for Raising Happy Healthy Children*

Once you have completed the Pregame Analysis, you have the information you need to make a **Game Plan** to change behavior. Now, it is time to think about what behavior you *want*. This is usually easy because it is the exact opposite of the sideliner. However, it is often a step that parents miss. Parents often do not tell their children what behavior they expect. Instead, they emphasize what they *do not* want. For example, "Stop hitting your brother," "Don't watch too much television," or "Quit yelling!" You should sit your child down, explain the behavior you want, and list the consequences of inappropriate behavior.

The purpose of this chapter is to choose the behavior you want and then develop a plan—a Game Plan—for teaching your child the behavior. The ABC model used in the Pregame Analysis is used again in the Game

Plan, with a twist for fun. By presenting the model as a game, your child is more likely to be interested. The more interested he or she is, the faster the behavior is likely to change.

In the Game Plan, antecedents become **strategies** for getting the desired behavior. The behavior you want is the **play**. When children make appropriate plays, they **score**. Scores then result in recognition and bonuses, which the ABC model calls consequences.

To make sure that change happens, this guide uses the following **Four Positive Behavior Boosters** to boost how often appropriate behavior occurs:

1. Identify the desired behavior. (What behavior do you want?)
2. Develop a plan to get the behavior. (How are you going to get it?)

3. Establish a plan to keep the behavior. (How are you going to keep getting it?)

4. Build a positive relationship with your child. (How are you going to build a relationship?)

The Game Plan uses the first three of the Four Positive Behavior Boosters. The Fourth Positive Behavior Booster will be discussed in Chapter 8.

The First Positive Behavior Booster

The first step in changing behavior is to describe the behavior you want in a way that is understandable to your child. You should focus on what your child needs to do.

It is important to teach a behavior that the child can learn. For example, your child may not be able to get all A's in school, so having this as a goal is not a good plan. A plan like this has unrealistic goals and sets everyone up for failure.

The behavior you want to teach should be the *opposite* of the Sideliner listed in the Pregame Analysis. The desired behavior is the **play** of the Game Plan. Examples of plays are completing homework, staying calm when upset, having a dry bed at night, and following instructions.

For example, Resistant Ralph was not following directions. In Ralph's Game Plan, the play would be "following directions in a certain period of time," as shown in Figure 8.

The Second Positive Behavior Booster

The second part of the Game Plan is to develop strategies. Strategies are what happens before the play to help your child make the play. You develop strategies using the Sideliner Analysis chart. By knowing what happens before the sideliner, you can create a plan to reduce the chance of getting the sideliner and increase the chance of getting the play.

The first strategy should be to explain the Game Plan to your child. (This strategy will be discussed in more detail in Chapter 7.) A common second strategy is to provide a nonverbal **reminder** when the player begins the sideliner. For example, if Ralph is still watching television after being asked to come to breakfast, one of his parents would give him a hand signal as a reminder. One example of a hand signal is to raise two fingers (but not point them at the player) without saying anything. If you feel angry, you should turn away and not make eye contact while giving the signal.

The strategies for Ralph's Game Plan are based on the items in the "Antecedents: What Happens Before?" column in his Sideliner Analysis chart. The strategies are to explain to Ralph in advance what will be expected of him, schedule television time, and provide only one reminder, such as a hand signal. Ralph's parents should also decide if Ralph needs to go to bed earlier the night before and get up earlier on the day he has responsibilities. Ralph's strategies are shown in Figure 9.

Nothing is particularly hard if you divide it into small jobs.

— Henry Ford

The Game Plan

Player: _Resistant Ralph_

Date: _2/25_

Strategies:
How to Get the Desired Behavior

Explain the Game Plan.

Give a hand signal.

The Play:
The Desired Behavior

Following directions in a certain period of time.

Recognition/Bonuses:
Reinforcing the Desired Behavior

Immediate Recognition:

Daily Bonuses:

Super Bonuses:

Penalties:

Figure 8

The Game Plan

Player: _____Resistant Ralph_____

Date: _____2/25_____

Strategies:
How to Get the Desired Behavior

Explain the Game Plan.

Give a hand signal when Ralph ignores directions. Practice the hand signal with Ralph.

Make one request at a time.

Warn Ralph to give him time to switch from one activity to another.

Be clear about when the task should be done.

Place a list on the refrigerator of tasks Ralph should finish by dinnertime.

Give no reminders other than the hand signal.

Do not debate with Ralph.

Ignore complaints.

The Play:
The Desired Behavior

Following directions in a certain period of time.

Recognition/Bonuses:
Reinforcing the Desired Behavior

Immediate Recognition:

Daily Bonuses:

Super Bonuses:

Penalties:

Figure 9

Going for the Gold

The Third Positive Behavior Booster

Now that you have decided what play to teach and the strategies you need to get that play, the Third Positive Behavior Booster is to decide how to keep getting the play. With the Game Plan, you give rewards when your child makes the play during a specified period of time. If there are any sideliners during the specified period of time, your child does not earn a reward. A sideliner that is stopped by a hand signal reminder does not result in the loss of a reward. When your child makes the correct play consistently, he or she earns scores, recognition, and bonuses. These rewards should cause your player to continue the positive behavior. Over time, your child can earn a **super bonus**, which is an extra special prize. The steps for the Third Positive Behavior Booster follow.

Step One: Recognition

The first reward in any Game Plan is for you (or another caregiver) to recognize the play. The recognition should include specific information about the play. For example, you, as coach, could say, "That was a difficult situation. You did a great job staying calm even though you were upset." Such recognition makes you part of your child's Booster Club and encourages your child to make more plays. The recognition should encourage your child to make the play again without other rewards. Your child should make the play to feel good about him or herself and to get attention for behaving correctly.

Recognition is important to increase the chance that the play will happen again. Positive comments help explain what you want, are always available, and can be delivered immediately without another reward. Parents should *always* give recognition—such as hugs, winks, smiles, nods of approval, pats on the back, and personal attention—for appropriate behavior.

Most communication is nonverbal (not spoken), meaning that people send messages through posture, facial expressions, and behavior. It is very important that your words match the messages you are sending with your body. If your words are positive but you are frowning, your child will probably pay more attention to your face than what you are saying.

You should also give recognition for each step toward the play, not just the play itself.

Step Two: Daily Bonuses

The **daily bonus** rewards your child for making the play and increases the possibility that he or she will repeat the play. Each day, your child can earn a daily bonus, such as phone or television privileges, for the next day. For example, if your child doesn't make the play on Tuesday, he or she will not earn the daily bonus for Wednesday.

The more often the sideliner occurs (as counted during the Pregame Analysis), the more often appropriate behavior must be rewarded. For example, if your child loses control an average of ten times a day, you might need to reward positive behavior every hour or two. If your child's sideliner is not completing homework or going to bed on time, rewarding once a day is enough.

Step Three: Super Bonuses

A super bonus is a special reward based on a certain number of plays. A super bonus is not something that happens every day. For example, your child could earn a trip to the zoo after making a total of ten plays. The super bonus should not occur more than once a week with perfect scores. If, at the end of the week, your child does not have enough scores to earn the super bonus, then the scores are carried over to the next week. As a result, if your child does not consistently make the plays, it will take longer to earn the super bonus.

Step Four: Penalties

Penalties are the opposite of recognition and bonuses. When your child does not make the play and earn a score, the penalty is the *loss* of recognition and bonuses. When angry, coaches often add a punishment to empha-

size the error. For example, if a child who was working on staying calm threw a tantrum at the grocery store, the angry parent might respond by dragging the child from the store or yelling. In this case, the parent gives a lot of negative attention to the child. Following the Game Plan, however, the parent would remain calm, remove the child from the store, and not give recognition or bonuses. No other penalty is added because the parent was especially angry or embarrassed. That would be a **double penalty**, which can ruin the entire Game Plan. A Game Plan is an agreement, and the purpose of this agreement is to teach your child that his or her behavior has consequences. By suddenly changing the Game Plan, you lose the chance to teach this important idea.

Appropriate Rewards and Penalties

Children must learn that there is a relationship between what they do and what happens to them. In the real world, there are generally no positive outcomes for inappropriate behavior. Likewise, your child should learn that simply being part of a family does not entitle him or her to television time, allowances, computers, stereos, telephones, pagers, and designer clothes. Instead, these privileges are connected to appropriate behavior. If your child is not doing his or her "job" in the game of life, then he or she has not earned the right to privileges.

Some parents think that offering rewards is bribery and should not be necessary for expected behavior. If their child has major behavior problems, however, the strategy of *not* offering rewards is not working. *All* behaviors that the child repeats are in some way being rewarded. Having a Game Plan is simply being *aware* of the behavior and how it is rewarded. It is important to keep this in mind when choosing rewards. The bonuses and super bonuses that you choose should flow naturally from the desired behavior.

It is important to choose rewards that your child wants. You may need to change the rewards frequently to keep your child interested in the game. There are two main types of rewards used with the Third Positive Behavior Booster: recognition and bonuses. Recognition was discussed earlier in this chapter.

Bonuses and Super Bonuses

Depending on their value system, some parents do not like to offer money as a bonus. Many children receive an allowance. Sometimes the allowance is earned, and sometimes it is not. Most children want money, and they will eagerly work for it. This begins to teach them how life works: most people have to work to earn money.

For children with behavior problems, money can be an important reward. If you use money as a bonus in the Game Plan, however, it is important not to give your child money outside the Game Plan. You also need to make sure that your child does not get money from relatives or other children. If your child wants to go to the movies but has not earned enough money for a ticket, you need to be sure he or she does not get the money to go from someone else. Money for school activities, such as field trips, should be paid for by you, not your child's earnings in the Game Plan.

If your child earns money as a reward in the Game Plan, you should not decide what he or she does with the money. Since your child earned the money, spending or saving it should be his or her choice. If your child wants to spend the money, forcing him or her to save it can destroy motivation and the results of the Game Plan.

Food is not recommended as a daily bonus, but it can be combined with a special trip for a super bonus. It is important that your child want the bonus enough to work for it. Starving your child to get good behavior is

never an option. Also, children should not learn to reward themselves with food, as it could result in weight problems later in life. There may be times, however, when food is the only thing that will get a response from some children, especially children with disabilities. In those cases, special food might be considered as a possible daily bonus.

Phone time, computer time, watching television, or playing video games are often good bonuses. A trip with a parent or another adult, such as lunch at a fast-food restaurant, provides time for special attention. The Game Plan helps ensure that you only give attention for appropriate behavior.

You should be careful when using extracurricular activities as rewards. Scouting, athletic teams, dance, or church groups are chances for your child to interact with people outside of school or home. The benefits of these activities outweigh the benefits of using them as rewards in the Game Plan.

In some cases, extracurricular activities take too much time away from other goals, such as studying. In many schools, participating in extracurricular activities is tied to grades and appropriate behavior, which are natural consequences separate from the Game Plan. For example, if a student does not have a certain grade point average, the school may not permit him or her to participate in athletic events or clubs.

Figure 10 gives some examples of good recognition, bonuses, and super bonuses that you can use with the Game Plan.

Punishment Vs. Discipline

Parents often want to punish bad behavior. Punishment—especially when delivered with a lot of emotion, such as spanking or yelling—is a bad example of what to do when

Types of Rewards

Recognition

Praise
Pats on the back
Smiles
High fives

Hugs
Winks
Nods of approval
Thumbs-up sign

Bonuses

Stickers
Riding bikes
Watching television
Talking on the telephone
Swimming

Money
Computer fun time
Playing video games
Playing with friends
Listening to the radio or CDs

Super Bonuses

Making brownies
Going out with parent(s)
Having a friend spend the night
Going out for an ice cream cone
Playing a board/card game with parent(s)
Picking out a video to rent
Earning doll clothes
Sleeping in a tent in the house
Buying a magazine or book
Going skating
Using the camera/video camera
Going to a sports game

Going to a fast-food restaurant
Going on a picnic
Spending the night with a relative
Choosing dinner
Going to a movie
Earning baseball cards
Staying up late on a weekend
Earning a CD
Going to the park
Going bowling
Taking a one-time class (i.e., cooking)
Having a lemonade stand

Going to a local attraction (i.e., carnivals, amusement parks, water parks)

Figure 10

angry, especially if the problem is that your child loses control when upset. Additionally, making an adult angry can be very rewarding for a child and he or she will probably repeat the behavior. Many children will risk a spanking to feel the power of controlling an adult's emotions. At the same time, parents often feel they are in control and teaching the child a lesson. In reality, however, the punishment may stop the behavior for a little while, which makes the adult feel better and in control, but the poor behavior usually occurs again. The problem with punishment is that it focuses on *stopping* inappropriate behavior, instead of *teaching* appropriate behavior.

When children misbehave, parents sometimes ground them "for life" and limit all privileges and activities. When this occurs, it is usually after the parent has told the child to do something many times and is at an "or else" point. When angry or upset, parents may give punishments that they will not carry out when they are calmer.

Grounding or time-outs for long periods of time do not work because misbehaving children need immediate feedback on their behavior. When they have a long-term punishment, children tend to forget why they are being punished and just become angry. At this point, parents often give in to the anger and discontinue the punishment, which teaches children that parents do not mean what they say. The next time, the children are likely to push their inappropriate behavior even further.

Examples: Resistant Ralph and Angry Agnes

The recognition and bonuses in Resistant Ralph's Game Plan are based on Ralph's favorite activities and interests. His parents decided the frequency of the rewards by how often the inappropriate behavior happened. Ralph's Frequency of Sideliner chart showed that Ralph ignored many directions each day. In order to change Ralph's behavior, his parents will need to break the day into parts and provide a score and a reward for each part.

In Resistant Ralph's case, his coaches divided the day into three parts: morning, afternoon, and evening. His parents knew that Ralph liked playing computer or video games. They decided that for each part of the day, Ralph could earn 30 minutes to play computer or video games the next day. After ten plays, Ralph could have a friend over for a super bonus. With perfect scores, Ralph could have a friend over almost every four days. When he reached 50 scores, Ralph could earn a movie with a snack.

If Ralph didn't make the play, his penalties were losing recognition, losing computer and video game time for the next day, taking longer to have a friend over, and taking longer to earn a movie and snack.

Completed Game Plans for Resistant Ralph and Angry Agnes are shown in Figures 11 and 12. Agnes's plan is similar to Ralph's, but has different rewards and bonuses.

Action: Completing the Game Plan

You are now ready to make a Game Plan for your player. Use the blank Game Plan chart in the Appendix and follow these steps:

1. Write the desired behavior or play, which is the opposite of the sideliner, in the middle column.

2. Write strategies for getting the play in the first column. Use your observations of what was happening before the sideliner occurred from the Sideliner Analysis chart.

3. In the third column, decide on recognition and daily bonuses and choose how often you will give them. Use the Frequency of Sideliner chart and what you believe your player will want. Choose a super bonus that will be a special treat for your player. You can change the bonuses and the super bonus later in the game if you need to *and* your player agrees.

4. At the bottom of the third column, write the penalties, which are loss of the recognition, bonuses, and super bonuses you decided on in step three.

The Game Plan

Player: _Resistant Ralph_

Date: _2/25_

Strategies:
How to Get the Desired Behavior

Explain the Game Plan.

Give a hand signal when Ralph ignores directions. Practice the hand signal with Ralph.

Make one request at a time.

Warn Ralph to give him time to switch from one activity to another.

Be clear about when the task should be done.

Place a list on the refrigerator of tasks Ralph should finish by dinnertime.

Give no reminders other than the hand signal.

Do not debate with Ralph.

Ignore complaints.

The Play:
The Desired Behavior

Following directions in a certain period of time.

Recognition/Bonuses:
Reinforcing the Desired Behavior

Immediate Recognition:
Praise Ralph when he follows directions in a certain period of time.

Daily Bonuses:
One score for each part of the day (morning, afternoon, and evening) without a sideliner. Each score equals 30 minutes of computer or video game time for the next day.

Super Bonuses:
10 scores equals having a friend over.

50 scores equals a movie at a theater with popcorn and a soda.

Penalties:
Loss of recognition when sideliner occurs.
Loss of attention when sideliner occurs.
Loss of score and resulting computer time.
Takes longer to earn having a friend over.
Takes longer to earn a movie and snack.

Figure 11

The Game Plan

Player: _Angry Agnes_

Date: _2/25_

Strategies:
How to Get the Desired Behavior

Explain the Game Plan.

Give a hand signal when Agnes begins to lose control.

Teach skills for staying calm when upset:
— Help Agnes identify how her body feels when she is upset.
— Have Agnes switch between tensing and relaxing her muscles.

Discuss situations that upset Agnes and how she can avoid them or remove herself.

Teach Agnes to think about something happy or fun when she is becoming upset.

Teach Agnes to take deep breaths, count to ten, and think "stay calm."

Act out situations and demonstrate the behavior you want to teach.

The Play:
The Desired Behavior

Staying calm when upset.

Recognition/Bonuses:
Reinforcing the Desired Behavior

Immediate Recognition:
Praise Agnes when she stays calm.

Daily Bonuses:
One score three times a day for remaining calm when upset. Each score equals 30 minutes of stereo/radio privileges or television time for the next day.

Super Bonuses:
15 scores equals staying overnight with grandmother.

30 scores equals $15 for a new CD.

Penalties:
Loss of recognition when sideliner occurs.

Loss of attention when sideliner occurs.

Loss of score and resulting stereo, radio, or television time.

Takes longer to earn staying overnight with grandmother.

Takes longer to earn a CD.

Figure 12

The Scoreboard

CHAPTER 6

Once you complete the Game Plan, write the information on the **Scoreboard**. The scoreboard is important because you will use it to chart scores and to explain the Game Plan to your player. The Scoreboard also shows at a glance how the player is doing each day, one week at a time. It can be hung on the refrigerator or inside a cupboard door. Use the Scoreboard in the Appendix and fill it in using these steps:

1. In "The Play" space, write the behavior you want (from the middle column of the Game Plan).

2. In the "Day of Week" row, write the day that the plan is starting in the first column. For example, if the plan is starting on Wednesday, write *Wednesday* in the first column and follow with the rest of the days of the week. On the Scoreboard, each day is divided into morning, afternoon, and evening. If you need to divide the day into more parts, mark the divisions on the Scoreboard. Your child earns one score for appropriate behavior during each division of time, whether it is part of the day or all of the day. For example, your child could earn one score for remaining calm all day, or three scores for remaining calm when the day is divided. At the end of the day, the scores earned each day are totaled in the "Total Score" row.

3. In the "Daily bonuses" section, describe what your player earns for making the play during each period of time during the day. For example, staying calm during a certain period of time results in earning television or phone time. Any displays of the sideliner means your child will not earn bonuses for *only* that period of time.

4. In the "Super bonuses" section, write what your player earns for a certain number of scores. For example, every time your player earns five scores, he or she earns a trip to a fast-food restaurant. Or, every time your player earns ten scores, he or she can have a friend over for the night. The scores do not have to be earned in a row or at the same time. Instead, super bonuses are based on collecting a certain number of scores, no matter how long it takes the player to get enough for the super bonus.

5. In the "Super bonus scores carried over from the previous week" section, write the scores that your player carried over from the last week *if* he or she has not reached the number needed for the super bonus. You will add new scores to these as they are earned.

Refer to the Scoreboards (Figures 13 and 14) for Resistant Ralph and Angry Agnes if you need help filling out a Scoreboard for your player. Scores for appropriate behavior are marked with checkmarks.

Scoreboard

Player: _____ Resistant Ralph _____

Week of: _____ 2/26–3/4 _____

The Play: _____ Following directions _____

Day of Week	Tuesday	Wednesday	Thursday	Friday	Saturday	Sunday	Monday
Morning		✓	✓	✓	✓		✓
Afternoon	✓	✓		✓	✓		✓
Evening		✓		✓	✓		
Total Score	1	3	1	3	3	0	2

Daily bonuses:

One score for each period of time that Ralph follows directions. Each score equals 30 minutes of computer or video game time for the next day.

Super bonuses:

10 scores earns having a friend over.

50 scores earns a movie at a theater with popcorn and a soda.

Super bonus scores carried over from the previous week:

3 scores carried over for having a friend over.

13 scores carried over for a movie at a theater with popcorn and a soda.

Figure 13

Scoreboard

Player: _____Angry Agnes_____

Week of: _____2/26-3/4_____

The Play: _____Staying calm when upset_____

Day of Week	Tuesday	Wednesday	Thursday	Friday	Saturday	Sunday	Monday
Morning	✓	✓	✓			✓	
Afternoon		✓	✓	✓	✓		✓
Evening	✓	✓					✓
Total Score	2	3	2	1	1	1	2

Daily bonuses:
Agnes can earn one score for staying calm when upset during each period of time. Each score equals 30 minutes of stereo, radio, or television time for the next day.

Super bonuses:
15 scores earns staying overnight with grandmother.
30 scores earns $15 for a new CD.

Super bonus scores carried over from the previous week:
5 scores carried over for staying overnight with grandmother.
5 scores carried over for a new CD.

Figure 14

The Game

Later in life, Winston Churchill was asked to give the commencement address at Oxford University. After he was introduced, he rose, went to the dais, and said, "Never, never, never give up." Then he took his seat.

— And I Quote

When the Game Plan and the Scoreboard are completed, it is time to start the game. An important part of the Game Plan is when you to explain it and the Scoreboard to your child. The best time may be the night before the game starts or when your player is in a good mood and energetic. You, as coach, must make sure that your player understands exactly how the Game Plan will work. To check for understanding, have your player explain the plan to you. It may be a good idea to try some role plays to help your child understand how the game will work. For example, if you will use a hand signal, you should practice the signal with your player.

It is important for coaches to be positive. For example, you should not tell your child that his or her allowance, television, stereo, or telephone privileges are being taken away. Instead, you should explain that the plan will teach your child how life works so he or she can prepare for growing up. One of the ways the plan will do that is to give your child privileges based on his or her behavior.

Your child may or may not buy into the plan. If he or she resists, have your child help choose the bonuses. It is helpful if your child agrees with the plan, but it does not really matter if he or she refuses to accept it. You should firmly state that this is how things will work now, then carry out the plan without arguing. If you have carefully analyzed your child's behavior and chosen bonuses that your child wants, the plan should eventually work, regardless of whether your child supports it.

If there are two parents in the home, both of you need to follow the plan. If possible, other caretakers also need to follow the plan.

Because it is very difficult to change behavior, you should use the plan for six months or more to make sure that the new behavior becomes a habit. Your child may need the plan for an even longer period of time, with changes in bonuses and super bonuses to keep your player interested.

If your child does not earn the recognition and bonuses, do not give them! You must follow the Game Plan with *absolute* consistency! Just as the rules of baseball or football do not change, neither should the Game Plan. For example, if you give a score when your child hasn't made a play, you will be rewarding the inappropriate behavior.

The plan may be interrupted because of a family emergency, such as an illness or a death. In these cases, you should continue the Game Plan as soon as possible and reward positive behavior even during the interruption.

If your child earns the recognition and bonuses, give them! Even if your child misbehaves in a way not covered in the Game Plan, he or she should still receive recognition and bonuses for plays in the plan. You can, however, give consequences for inappropriate behavior not covered by the Game Plan. The consequences should have to do with the poor behavior, not the Game Plan penalties.

Away Games

Consistency is important to the success of the plan. If you and your child's other parent share custody, it is helpful if both of you use the plan. However, if the other parent does not want to carry out the plan, don't make an issue of it. Although consistency is great, your child can learn that there are different rules for different places.

The Game Plan focuses on your child's behavior while you, the parent, are watching. When

your child is at school, he or she automatically earns a score for that period of time. If there are problems at school, you should deal with them outside of the Game Plan. For example, if a teacher calls home regarding your child's behavior at school, you can choose to punish the child for this, but separately from the Game Plan. For example, your child might not be able to play with friends for the next two evenings, *if* this penalty is not a part of the Game Plan.

In some cases, you may ask the school for help with the plan. Some teachers might be willing to provide recognition when your player makes plays at school. This support will help your player learn to control his or her behavior in different places. Sideliners at school, however, should not affect the Game Plan at home. If you wish, you can make another plan to deal with sideliners at school. This Game Plan should have different rewards than the Game Plan at home. The rewards could be provided at home, at school, or both.

Problems With the Game

As you carry out the Game Plan, problems can develop. Even though it is not possible to list all the problems that may happen, here are some of the more common ones.

Rebellion When There Is No Score

When your player does not earn a bonus, he or she may get upset. You need to remember to stay calm and follow the Game Plan; recognition and bonuses are not given if your child does not earn them. You should not make comments or judgments when your player does not earn the score. For example, if your player had a good day until 7 P.M. and then lost control, he or she does not earn a score for the evening, in spite of the earlier good behavior. You must not give in if your player demands or begs for a score because of the earlier good behavior. You should tell your player that the Game Plan (not you) says there was no score. This way, you remove responsibility from yourself if your child does not earn a bonus. Separating yourself from your child's behavior helps put the responsibility on your child. If your child continues to negotiate or beg, you should calmly walk away and do something else, while ignoring your child. This response does not reward the nagging because no attention is given to your child. It also shows your child how to handle pestering in his or her life.

Power Struggles

Power struggles can become a big problem between a child and parent. Some children will go to great lengths to be sure that an adult never wins a power struggle. If your child wants to misbehave, especially as he or she gets older and you have less control, he or she will usually find a way to do it. For example, if your child wants to upset you by getting poor grades, he or she will lose homework, even though it is completed, on the way to school.

In the case of a power struggle, you must continue to follow the Game Plan with as little emotion as possible. Your child will suffer other natural consequences to his or her behavior.

Testing Limits

You should realize that most children test their limits. When the Game Plan starts, your player may respond well for a while before beginning to test you. After a period of success, your player will begin to wonder what would happen if he or she did not behave correctly. Could he or she earn a reward even if there was a sideliner and no score?

When and if your player challenges the plan: be prepared! Just when you begin to relax and feel success, the sideliner may increase until it is worse than before the Game Plan. Your player will try to get you to go back to the way things were before, when your player got what he or she wanted without having to earn it. Of course, you may be surprised at this change and may even begin to question whether the plan will work at all.

The only way to deal with this situation is to ignore the sideliner and carry on with the plan. When your player discovers that the only way to get what he or she wants is to earn it, then he or she will go back to the plan. Your child may challenge the plan several times. Always remember to stick to the plan!

Time-Outs

When your child becomes out of control and risks harming him or herself or others, you must take action. At such times, you should avoid showing emotion or giving your child a lot of attention. Your child can be put in

The only way to get the best of an argument is to avoid it.

— Dale Carnegie

time-out until his or her behavior improves. The shorter the time-out, the better. Three or four minutes is usually enough. The time-out should be in a place where your child is safe and has nothing else to do. At first, the out-of-control behavior may last longer but, if you ignore it, it should eventually stop. Once your child understands that the Game Plan is not going away, the sideliner will decrease again.

The Fourth Positive Behavior Booster

CHAPTER 8

To relate effectively ... we must learn to listen. And this requires emotional strength. Listening involves patience, openness, and the desire to understand—highly developed qualities of character. It's so much easier to operate from a low emotional level and to give high level advice.

— Steven R. Covey, *The Seven Habits of Highly Effective People*

In the Game Plan, your focus is on replacing sideliners with appropriate behavior. Coaching children in the game of life involves more than just sideliners. The Fourth Positive Behavior Booster moves beyond improving behavior to improving your relationship with your child. It involves two techniques that you, as a coach, should use at the same time as the Game Plan: **Spotlighting the Positive** and **Daily Connecting**. These two techniques will help your child play well in the game of life.

Spotlighting the Positive

In the Game Plan, you recognize the desired behavior every time it occurs and give scores at the end of certain time periods. At the same time, you should also recognize other positive behavior. By **spotlighting** all appropriate behavior, it increases the chance that your child will repeat them. Recognizing both the play and other appropriate behaviors goes beyond the benefits of the plan to go for the gold.

When working to change a problem behavior, it may seem as if there are few, if any, occasions for recognition. Catching your child being good in order to give recognition may be a challenge. With practice it will become easier and should eventually become a habit.

Positive feedback is important because too much negative feedback can cause your child to think badly of him or herself and form a "why bother" attitude, which is hard to change. Once this happens, your child is not

Novice golfer to husband, teeing off: "Now tell me if you notice anything I'm doing right."

— And I Quote

likely to accept positive feedback, because he or she does not believe it.

Spotlighting should be positive, genuine, and uplifting so your child feels complimented. If you say positive words, such as "way to go," with sarcasm, then you are zinging, not spotlighting. Your child will remember the negative, not the positive, part of the comment, which could hurt his or her progress toward better behavior. When spotlighting appropriate behaviors, you should avoid adding a zinger, such as "I appreciate it when you hang your clothes up, but it would be helpful if you put your dirty clothes in the hamper." See Figure 15 for more examples of accidental zingers.

Spotlighting is a powerful force in changing behavior. Children need to receive at least five times more positive than negative feedback.

This feedback helps them learn appropriate behavior and develop a healthy self-image. Giving attention to *any* type of behavior will increase the occurrence of that behavior. If the focus is on negative behavior, more negative behavior will happen. If focus is on positive behavior, more positive behavior will happen.

By going back to the Frequency of Recognition/Zingers chart, you can analyze your tendency to spotlight. Spotlighting can be hard because it is easier to focus on correcting inappropriate behavior. However, research consistently shows that the best way to change behavior is to reward appropriate behavior. Once you carry out a Game Plan and increase spotlighting, your child's other problem behaviors outside the Game Plan often improve.

Spotlighting	Zinging
Wow, you got a "B" on your test, good job . . .	If you study harder, maybe you can get an "A" next time.
I really like the shirt you picked out . . .	But it looks awful with those pants.
I liked the way you were sharing with Mary this afternoon . . .	Too bad you don't do that with your brother.
Thanks for helping clear the table tonight . . .	Maybe I wouldn't be so tired at night if you helped more around the house.
I appreciate it when you get home on time . . .	Too bad you can't do it with a smile on your face.
Your dad says you keep your room really clean at his house . . .	I guess you care more about what he thinks than what I think.
I like how you are spending less time on the phone . . .	If only you would use the time to study instead of watch television.

Figure 15

Going for the Gold

Daily Connecting

The point of Daily Connecting is to build a quality relationship between you and your player. It is a time for your player to talk about anything, without any judgments from you. It is a time for your player to choose a topic and for you to listen. It is not a time for lecturing, instructing, teaching, or talking about the Game Plan, unless your player brings it up.

During Daily Connecting, you connect to your player by actively listening. In active listening, you listen to your player with few or no interruptions, such as phone calls. You show your player that you understand by rephrasing what your player has said. You should not tell your player if you agree or disagree with what he or she has said. Instead, you should ask questions to get more information or gently broaden the player's thinking. Your nonverbal communication, such as posture or eye contact, should show that you are focused on your player and what he or she is saying.

Daily Connecting can be hard to start. At first, your child may not like Daily Connecting. You should find a time when your child is interested in talking. The time when your child wants to talk about something may not always be the best time for you to stop and listen. Similarly, when you have time to listen, your child may not want to talk. A good time for Daily Connecting is when both you and your child are relaxed and there are few interruptions.

Many children, especially older children, want to talk when coaches cannot make eye contact, such as when cooking or riding in the car. You may be physically, but not mentally, busy so you can connect with your child. Children often resist talking to their parents because they fear lectures, arguments, judgments, overreactions, or parents who want to solve problems instead of just listening. As you show active listening skills, your child will become easier to talk to and more likely to

CHANNELS
Channel 1's no fun.
Channel 2's just news.
Channel 3's hard to see.
Channel 4 is just a bore.
Channel 5 is all jive.
Channel 6 needs to be fixed.
Channel 7 and Channel 8—
Just old movies, not so great.
Channel 9's a waste of time.
Channel 10 is off, my child.
Wouldn't you like to <u>talk</u> awhile?

— Shel Silverstein, *A Light in the Attic*

tell you what he or she is thinking and feeling. Ideally, you should try to talk with your child for at least fifteen minutes each day.

If done every day, Daily Connecting sets the stage for a lifetime of good communication between you and your child. If you hope to be the person your child turns to when there is a problem, you need to build a trusting relationship now. This relationship cannot be put off until you have more time. Because Daily Connecting improves the relationship between you and your child, it may turn out to be the most important time you ever spend with your child.

Final Thoughts

To coach your child in the game of life, you must teach the plays necessary for good relationships. The Game Plan in this guide focuses on a certain behavior. You tell your child what you expect and help him or her learn to connect behavior to results. As your child sees that appropriate behavior brings rewards, the appropriate behavior will increase in all areas, not just the area being specifically taught. The Game Plan also removes the stress of deciding how you will handle misbehavior. Using the Four Positive Behavior Boosters should decrease stress and improve family relationships, which helps you support your child in life. By spotlighting positive behavior and using Daily Connecting, you can improve the relationship between you and your child.

When you spend less time on problem behavior, you can spend more time on activities that build character and develop areas of strengths and interest. This plan truly moves parenting toward going for the gold.

Sideliner Analysis

Player: _____

Date: _____

Antecedents: What Happens Before?	Behavior	Consequences: What Happens After?

Frequency of Sideliner

Player: _____

Week of: _____

Day of Week							
Total							

Frequency of Recognition/Zingers

Coach: _____

Player: _____

Week of: _____

	Monday	Tuesday	Wednesday	Thursday	Friday	Saturday	Sunday	Total
Recognition								
Zingers								

44

The Game Plan

Player: _____

Date: _____

Strategies:
How to Get the Desired Behavior

Explain the Game Plan.

Give a hand signal.

The Play:
The Desired Behavior

Recognition/Bonuses:
Reinforcing the Desired Behavior

Immediate Recognition:

Daily Bonuses:

Super Bonuses:

Penalties:

Scoreboard

Player: _____

Week of: _____

The Play: _____

Day of Week						
Morning						
Afternoon						
Evening						
Total Score						

Daily bonuses:

Super bonuses:

Super bonus scores carried over from the previous week:

46

Applewhite, Ashton, William R. Evans III, and Andrew Frothingham. 1992. *And I quote*. New York, NY: St. Martin's Press.

Blechman, Elaine A. 1985. *Solving child behavior problems at home and at school*. Champaign, IL: Research Press.

Covey, Steven R. 1989. *The seven habits of highly effective people*. New York, NY: Simon & Schuster.

Glenn, H. Stephen, and Jane Nelsen. 1987. *Raising children for success*. Fair Oaks, CA: Sunrise Press.

Nelsen, Jane. 1987. *Positive discipline*. New York, NY: Ballantine Books.

Nelsen, Jane. 1999. *Positive time-out*. Rocklin, CA: Prima Publications.

Patterson, Gerald R. 1976. *Living with children*. Champaign, IL: Research Press.

Rosemond, John. 1989. *Six-point plan for raising happy, healthy children*. Kansas City, MO: Andrews and McMeel.

———. 1990. *Ending the homework hassle*. Kansas City, MO: Andrews and McMeel.

Rudner, Rita. 2000. Performance at the MGM Hotel and Casino. Las Vegas, NV, August.

Silverstein, Shel. 1981. *A light in the attic*. New York, NY: Harper & Row.